Landforms

Valleys

Cassie Mayer

Heinemann
LIBRARY

www.heinemann.co.uk/library
Visit our website to find out more information about **Heinemann Library** books.

To order:
☎ Phone 44 (0) 1865 888066
🖹 Send a fax to 44 (0) 1865 314091
💻 Visit the Heinemann Bookshop at www.heinemann.co.uk/library to browse our
catalogue and order online.

First published in Great Britain by Heinemann Library,
Halley Court, Jordan Hill, Oxford OX2 8EJ, part of
Harcourt Education.Heinemann is a registered trademark
of Harcourt Education Ltd.

Editorial: Tracey Crawford, Cassie Mayer, Dan Nunn,
  and Sarah Chappelow
Design: Jo Hinton-Malivoire
Picture Research: Ruth Blair
Production: Duncan Gilbert

Originated by Chroma Graphics (Overseas) Pte. Ltd
Printed and bound in China by South China
Printing Company

10 digit ISBN 0 431 18232 9
13 digit ISBN 978 0 431 18232 2

11 10 09 08 07
10 9 8 7 6 5 4 3 2 1

British Library Cataloguing in Publication Data
Mayer, Cassie
  Valleys. - (Landforms)
  1.Valleys - Juvenile literature
  I.Title
  551.4'42
A full catalogue record for this book is available from the
British Library.

Acknowledgements
The publishers would like to thank the following for
permission to reproduce photographs:
Alamy pp. **10** (Jon Arnold Images), **15** (Leslie Garland
Picture Library); Corbis pp. **4** (mountain, Royalty Free;
volcano, Galen Rowell; island, George Steinmetz), **5** (Pat
O'Hara), **6** (Richard Klune), **7** (Pat O'Hara), **11** (Jon
Sparks), **12** (Keren Su), **13** (Franz Marc Frei), **14**, **16**
(Royalty Free), **17** (Dean Conger), **19** (Pablo Corral Vega),
21 (Ashley Cooper), **22** (river, Royalty-Free; rhino, Alissa
Crandall; village, Keren Su); Getty Images pp. **8**
(PhotoDisc), **9** (PhotoDisc), **18** (John Lawrence), **20**
(Kate Thompson).

Cover photograph of clouds over the Aniscio Canyon
reproduced with permission of Corbis/Francesc Muntada.
Backcover image of the Hooker Valley, New Zealand
reproduced with permission of Corbis/Franz Marc Frei.

Every effort has been made to contact copyright holders
of any material reproduced in this book. Any omissions
will be rectified in subsequent printings if notice is given
to the publishers.

Contents

Landforms

The land is made of different shapes.
These shapes are called landforms.

valley

A valley is a landform.
Valleys are found all over the world.

What is a valley?

A valley is low land between hills and mountains.

In a mountain range there are valleys between each mountain.

Many streams flow down the high mountains. The streams join up and become a river.

The river flows between the hills.
Over a long time, the river wears the
rock away. A valley is formed.

Valleys change shape over time.

Most rivers flow down the valleys and into the sea. This river flows down a valley and forms a lake.

Types of valleys

Some valleys are steep and narrow.

This valley has steep sides.
It is shaped like a "V".

Some valleys are flat and wide.

This valley is shaped like a "U".
It was formed by a river of ice.

Some valleys are called canyons.
This river has cut through the rock to
form a deep canyon.

Some valleys have wide, slow-moving rivers flowing through them.

What lives in a valley?

Plants and animals live in valleys.
Trees and bushes grow beside the river.

People grow crops in valleys.
They also keep their animals in valleys.

Visiting valleys

People like to visit valleys.
Some people like to walk beside
the river.

Valleys show us the highs and lows
of the land.

Valley facts

A canyon is a type of valley. The Grand Canyon in the USA is the largest canyon in the world.

The Great Rift Valley is in Africa. It is home to many different animals.

Picture glossary

steep almost straight up

and down

Index

Notes to parents and teachers

Before reading

Talk about valleys. Explain that they are landforms which are formed between hills or mountains. Talk about how streams and rivers wear away the rock and over a long time the valley is made deeper and wider. Explain that rain and melted snow pour down the mountainside, through the valley and out into a lake or the sea.

After reading

Make a model valley. Help the children to use plasticine to make two steep-sided mountains. Roll a flat bed of plasticine to be the valley bottom and curve it up to the base of the mountains. Score out of the mountain sides channels for the water to flow down. Then make a wider channel for the water to flow through the valley. Place a shallow lid at the mouth of the river to collect the water. Gently pour water down the mountainside and observe how it flows into the valley and down into the "lake".

Mountains and Valleys Game: Label an area of the hall "The Sea". Tell the children that when you call out "Mountain" they have to find a partner and make an arch as high as they can. When you call out "Valley" they have to crouch down as low as they can. When you call out "The Sea" all the children have to run to the area marked "The Sea".

Titles in the *Landforms* series include:

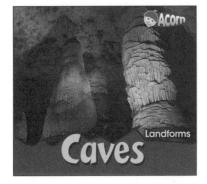

Caves

Hardback   0 431 18230 2

Islands

Hardback   0 431 18233 7

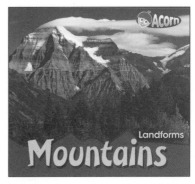

Mountains

Hardback   0 431 18231 0

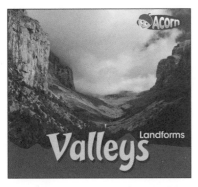

Valleys

Hardback   0 431 18232 9

Volcanoes

Hardback   0 431 18234 5

Find out about other titles from Heinemann Library on our website www.heinemann.co.uk/library